Good for You!

Toddler Rhymes for Toddler Times

original rhymes by **Stephanie Calmenson**

pictures by **Melissa Sweet**

HarperCollinsPublishers

Good for You!

"Letter Parade!": A slightly different version originally appeared in *Bug in a Rug*, published by Morrow Junior Books.
"Who Said, 'Moo'?": A prose version was originally published under the same title by Marvel Books.
"At the Playground": The untitled third stanza (swing) originally appeared in *What Am I?*, published by HarperCollins Children's Books.

www.harperchildrens.com
Library of Congress Cataloging-in-Publication Data
Calmenson, Stephanie.
Good for you! : toddler rhymes for toddler times / original rhymes by Stephanie Calmenson / pictures by Melissa Sweet.
p. cm.
ISBN 0-688-17737-9 — ISBN 0-06-029811-1 (lib. bdg.)
1. Children's poetry, American. [1. American poetry.]
I. Sweet, Melissa, ill. II. Title.
PS3553.A425 G66 2001
811'.54—dc21 00-040891 CIP AC
Typography by Stephanie Bart-Horvath
1 2 3 4 5 6 7 8 9 10
❖
First Edition

Dear Reader,

This book was written just for you.
You can listen to rhymes. Look at pictures, too.

Play peekaboo with colors. Parade with *A, B, C.*
You can sing. You can dance. You can count past three.

There's a bath with bubbles.
There's a bear with troubles.

There are kittens and puppies and cows and ducks.
There are bumpity buses, fire engines, and trucks.

There's lots to see and lots to do.
Can *you* turn the pages? You can? Good for you!

Contents

Peekaboo! I See Blue! 6

Knock, Knock! 13

First Things 14

At the Playground 16

Bumpity Bus 18

Fire Truck 19

Oops! Excuse Me! 20

Things We Do 21

I'm a Very Noisy Person! 28

I'm a Very Quiet Person 29

Nose to Toes 30

Traffic Jam 34

Who Said, "Moo"? 40

Tumble! Rumble! 42
Letter Parade! 44
My Room 46
My Potty 48
Look at Me! 49
Riding in My Stroller 50
Wag, Hop, Hide! 54
Teddy Bear Eats Out 56
Hello, Soap! 60
The Sleepy Clock 61
Good for You! 62
About the Author
About the Artist 64

Peekaboo! I See Blue!

Sam wants to play.
Will you play, too?
The name of the game
Is peekaboo.

Peekaboo! I see **blue**!
Blue ball, blue floor.
Blue cat at the door.

Peekaboo! I see **yellow**.
Yellow soap. Yellow boat.
Yellow duck. See them float?

Peekaboo! I see **red**.
Red truck, red blocks,
Red fox in a box.

Peekaboo! I see **green**.
Green rug, green tree,
Green frog on TV.

Peekaboo, colors!
Green, **red**, **yellow**, **blue**.
Peekaboo! I see you!

There are lots more colors.
But wait, where's Sam?

Peekaboo! Here I am!

Knock, Knock!

Knock, knock.
Who's there?
Grandma Jennie!

Knock, knock.
Who's there?
Grandpa Joe.

Knock, knock.
Who's there?
Aunt Melissa.

Knock, knock.
Who's there?
Uncle Moe.

Knock, knock.
Who's there?
Cousin Artie.

Knock, knock.
Who's there?
Pizza! Party!

First Things

Here's my first haircut.
Don't I look nice?

Here's my first picture.
Look! I drew it twice!

Here's my first toothbrush.
My teeth are clean. See?

Here's my first boo-boo.
I fell and scraped my knee.

Here's my first costume.
See my whiskers and my tail.

Here's my first letter.
Grandma sent it in the mail.

Here's my first party.
On my birthday I turned one.

Here's my first friend.
I like him. We have fun.

At the Playground

Bring a shovel you can dig with
And a bucket you can fill.
I'm flat and full of something fun
To sprinkle, pour, and spill.
What am I?

Sandbox

Climb my ladder
Up to the top,
Then sail back down—
WHEEE!—till you stop.
What am I?

Slide

I hang from a bar,
Or sometimes a tree.
Ask a friend for a push
When you ride on me.
What am I?

Swing

I can spin around fast,
Or glide around slow.
Sit down. Hold tight.
And away we go!
What am I?

Merry-go-round

Bumpity Bus

Bumpity, bumpity, bumpity bus.
Will you please stop for us?

Run, run! Catch the bus!
Run, run! It stopped for us!

Climb inside.
Pay for our ride.

Bumpity, bumpity, bumpity bus.
Now we're riding. Good for us!

Fire Truck

Clang! Clang!
Fire truck coming!
Racing down the street.
Fire in a building.
Feel the heat!

Jump from the truck.
Connect the hose.
Whoosh! Whoosh! Whoosh!
There the water goes.

The people are safe.
So is the cat.
The fire is out.
How about that!

Oops! Excuse Me!

When a hungry mouse wants your cheese,
Does she say, "May I have some, *please*?"

If you give a puppy a bone to chew,
Does he say, "I love it! *Thank you!*"

If a pig muddies your shirt and you need to clean it,
Does she say, "*I'm sorry.* I didn't mean it!"

When a giraffe stands up and you can't see,
Does he say, "Oops! *Excuse me!*"

Do animals have good manners?
No, I don't think they do.
But *you* can have good manners.
Will you try? Good for you!

Things We Do

Here are Anna and Brad,
And Michael and Sue.
Look at the things
That they can do.

At breakfast Michael
Picks his spoon up,
Eats some cereal,
Drinks from his cup.

Sue helps pick out
The clothes she'll wear.
Today she has a
Red bow in her hair.

Brad helps care for
His dog named Pete.
He brushes his coat,
Then gives him a treat.

Anna and Daddy
Go to the store.
Anna likes apples,
So they buy four.

Michael curls up
In a chair to look
At pictures in
His favorite book.

Anna drives her
Brand-new car.
Zoom! Zoom-zoom!
She goes far!

Brad likes drawing
Pictures a lot.
Crayon on paper.
Line, squiggle, dot!

Together these friends
Run, jump, climb.
They're busy almost
All the time!

Now you know what
They can do.
Are these the things
That *you* do, too?

I'm a Very Noisy Person!

I'm a very noisy person.
Yes, I am! Yes, I am!

I can clap my hands.
Clap, clap! Clap, clap!

I can sing a song.
La, la! La, la!

I can knock sticks together.
Bam, bam! Bam, bam!

I can ring a bell.
Dingdong! Dingdong!

I can stamp my feet.
Stamp, stamp! Stamp, stamp!

I'm a very noisy person.
Yes, I am! Yes, I am! Yes, I am!

I'm a Very Quiet Person

I'm a very quiet person.
Yes, I am. Yes, I am.

I can whisper very softly.
Psst-psst. Psst-psst.

I can sit and read a book.
Turn the page. Turn the page.

I can walk so you can't hear me.
Tiptoe. Tiptoe.

I can rock my doll to sleep.
Hush-a-bye. Hush-a-bye.

I'm a very quiet person.
Yes, I am. Yes, I am. Yes, I am.

Nose to Toes

I have one on my face.
You have one too.
This part is for smelling,
And sneezing—achoo!
What is it?

Nose

This is the place
Where food goes in.
It's below my nose
And above my chin.
What is it?

Mouth

I have two of these.
I use them to see.
When I look in the mirror,
I can see me!
What are they?

Eyes

With both of these
I listen well
To my barking dog,
Or a ringing bell.
What are they?

Ears

Each one can hold things.
Together they clap.
I wave them in the air,
Or rest them in my lap.
What are they?

Hands

They're part of my feet.
I wiggle them and then
I count them all up.
Do you see? I have ten!
What are they?

Toes

From nose to toes,
The parts fit well.
They make a person.
Who is it? Can you tell?

Me!

Traffic Jam

My car broke down
So here I am.
I just started
A traffic jam!

Putt, putt.

I wish right now
That I could float
Along a river
On a boat.

I wish that I could
Fly a plane . . .

Or cross a bridge
On a train.

I wish so much
I was not stuck.
Wait! Look what's here. . . .
It's a big tow truck!

Hook me up!
Tow me away!
There's no more
Traffic jam today.

Who Said, "Moo"?

I went to a farm when I was two,
And on that farm, I heard a "Moo!"

Who said, "Moo"? Horse, did you?
No way! Horse said, "Neigh!"

Who said, "Moo"? Lamb, did you?
No, ha-ha! Lamb said, "Baa!"

Who said, "Moo"? Cat, did you?
He didn't know how. Cat said, "Meow!"

Who said, "Moo"? Dog, did you?
That would be tough. Dog said, "Ruff!"

Who said, "Moo"? Hen, did you?
No such luck. Hen said, "Cluck!"

I was feeling so sad,
I wanted to cry,
When a black-and-white cow
Came walking by.

Do you know what she said?
I think you do.
Let's say it together:
The cow said, *"MOOOO!"*

Tumble! Rumble!

1 block
2 blocks
3 blocks
In a row.

4 blocks
5 blocks
6 blocks—
Up they go.

7 blocks
8 blocks
9 blocks
Going high.

10 blocks
11 blocks
12 blocks—
Oh, my!

Tumble!
Rumble!
Blocks in
A jumble!

Letter Parade!

Hello, *A!* Hello, *B!*
Everyone wave to the letter *C!*

I like those smiles, *D and E.*
Very lively, *F* and *G.*

H and *I,* you must not play.
"March like us!" say *J* and *K.*

L, M, N, you've got the beat!
O and *P,* lift up those feet!

Q, you're tripping! Tie your laces.
R, S, T, please find your places!

Excellent marching, *U* and *V.*
Good for you, *W, X, Y,* and *Z!*

HIJK
LMNOP
Q RST
UVWXYZ

My Room

Come in my room. Meet my bear.
He's sitting in my rocking chair.

There's my bed.
My blanket's red.

My yellow box
Is filled with blocks.

See the pictures on my wall?
Some are big. Some are small.

Toot! Toot! That's my train!
I have a car, a boat, a plane.

I love my dolls. One is new.
Do you have dolls that you love, too?

In my room I dance! I sing!
I make up songs about everything!

Here's my reading rug. I'll get a book.
This is my room. Come in. Take a look.

My Potty

I have my own potty.
I use it very well.
When I need the potty,
I can almost always tell.

I sit down on the potty.
I use it till I'm through.
I wipe. I flush. I wash my hands.
Have you a potty, too?

Look at Me!

Arms go in the sweater.
Legs go in the pants.
I try to do it right,
But sometimes I just can't.

My pants get on my arms,
My legs get in my sweater.
I try and try again.
I want to do it better.

Look at me! Do you see?
I got myself all dressed.
I really, really did it!
Don't I look the best?

Riding in My Stroller

I'm riding in my stroller.
What do I see?
Two friendly people who are
Waving at me.
I wave back.

I'm riding in my stroller.
What do I hear?
Trucks and cars honking
Right in my ear!
Honk! Honk!

I'm riding in my stroller.
Who trots past?
A big, happy dog who is
Going so fast!
Woof!

I'm riding in my stroller.
What do I do?
Kick, kick, kick,
There goes my shoe.
I used to have two.

I'm riding in my stroller,
Singing my own song.
We go into a market and
The fruit man sings along.
Dee, dee-da-dum, dee-dum!

I'm riding in my stroller,
Getting sleepy as can be.
Now my eyes are closing.
It's nap time for me.
Shhh.

Wag, Hop, Hide!

Puppies wag.

Bunnies hop.

Kittens pounce.

Don't stop!

Birds flap.

Bugs crawl.

Turtles hide.

We do it all!

Teddy Bear Eats Out

I'm taking Teddy to a restaurant.
It will be a special treat.
I say, "Remember, when we get there,
Please behave yourself and eat."

Our table's by the door.
Lots of people walking by.
Teddy's very noisy.
When they pass him, he yells, "Hi!"

While I'm looking at the menu,
Teddy's busy in his chair.
Soon there's no more salt or pepper,
And there's ketchup everywhere!

The waitress brings us water.
Teddy asks her for a straw.
When she brings him one,
Teddy asks her for some more.

He blows bubbles in the water,
Then he takes a little sip,
And he coughs and he dribbles,
And the glass begins to tip!

At last the food arrives.
We get toast and eggs and cheese.
Teddy turns his head away.
I say, "Take one bite, Teddy, please?"

So he tastes the eggs and cheese.
Then he takes a bite of toast.
Yum! Going to a restaurant
Is what Teddy likes the most!

Hello, Soap!

Splash! Soak.
Spill. Tip.
Sink. Float.
Pop! Drip.

Dunk. Squeeze.
Fill. Pour.
Does anyone know what
I'm in the tub for?

Oh, yes. Hello, soap!
Hi, shampoo!
I guess I have some
Washing to do.

The Sleepy Clock

Tick, tock. Tick, tock.
Listen to the sleepy clock.
"It's time for bed,"
The clock has said.

Tuck your blanket to your chin.
Cozy up. Snuggle in.
Give a hug. Get a kiss.
We like to go to bed like this.

Tick, tock. Tick, tock.
Listen to the sleepy clock.
Tick, tock. Tick, tock.
Tick. Tock. Tick.

Good for You!

You talk on the phone.
You comb your hair.
You set the table.
You hug your bear.
You sweep the floor.
You put toys away.
You help bake a cake.
You have friends come to play.
There are so many things
That you can do.
Take a big bow.
Good for you!

Stephanie Calmenson and her dog, Rosie

About the Author

Stephanie Calmenson loves to write for children. Her books have been called "marvelous" (*Publishers Weekly*), "lyrical" (*School Library Journal*), "sweet, funny, and right on the mark" (ALA *Booklist*). Some of her most popular titles include *Dinner at the Panda Palace,* a PBS Storytime Book; *The Principal's New Clothes; The Frog Principal; The Teeny Tiny Teacher;* and *Rosie, a Visiting Dog's Story,* the true story of her dog, Rosie, who went to dog school so she could cheer up people who are sad or sick or lonely. Good for Stephanie and Rosie!

Before becoming a writer, Stephanie was a teacher and a children's book editor. She lives in New York City. You can read more about her at her website: www.stephaniecalmenson.com.

Melissa Sweet and her cat, Rosie

About the Artist

Melissa Sweet has received universal praise for her "fetching watercolors" (ALA *Booklist*), "sunny art" (*The Bulletin of the Center for Children's Books*), and "delectable paintings" (*Publishers Weekly* starred review), which have appeared in *Dirty Laundry Pile: Poems in Different Voices,* selected by Paul B. Janeczko; *Bouncing Time,* by Patricia Hubbell; *Will You Take Care of Me?* by Margaret Park Bridges; and Kathi Appelt's *Bats Around the Clock, Bats on Parade,* and *Bat Jamboree.*

Since she was a child, Melissa has been drawing, painting, and working with her hands. "In my family, everyone was always busy making things. If we wanted something, we made it. Even our toys were made of wood."

Melissa lives with Mark, Emily, Arista, and a myriad of cats in Rockport, Maine.